Thank you for choosing our coloring book and supporting our small business!

We trust you'll enjoy your coloring journey. The entire team behind this book is grateful for your patronage.

We'd be delighted if you could leave a review. Your feedback sustains our livelihood.

Feel free to showcase your vibrant creations on our Amazon page!

Copyright 2024 Lara Frost
All rights reserved. This book or any portion there of may not be reproduced or used in any manner whatsoever without the publisher's express written permission except for the use of brief quotations in a book review.
First Printing, 2024

COLORING TIPS & TRICKS

1) Our paper is most suited for colored pencils, crayons, pastels and alcohol-based markers. Experiments with different shading techniques and textures to create your own unique style!

2) In addition to being a great stress-reducer and relaxation activity, coloring can also be a fun way to connect with others. Share your finished pages on social media with hashtag #lizziemalonecoloring!

3) To protect upcoming pages, we recommend placing a blank piece of paper under the page you're working on.

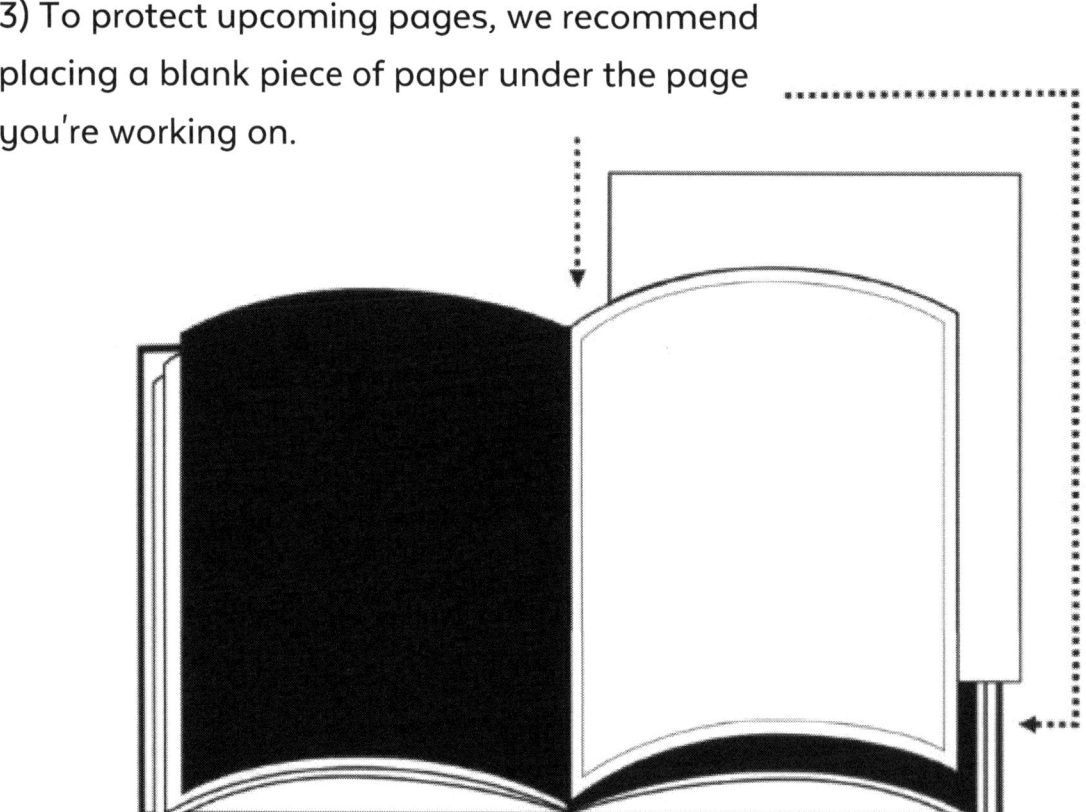